VOL 3

# CLIMATE CHRONICLES

## TURN YOUR BACKYARD INTO A SECRET FOREST

MOONSTONE

Published in Moonstone
by Rupa Publications India Pvt. Ltd 2024
7/16, Ansari Road, Daryaganj
New Delhi 110002

Sales centres:
Bengaluru Chennai
Hyderabad Jaipur Kathmandu
Kolkata Mumbai Prayagraj



P-ISBN: 978-93-6156-851-0
E-ISBN: 978-93-6156-604-2

First impression 2024

10 9 8 7 6 5 4 3 2 1

Printed in India

# Contents

# Contents

# DEFORESTATION AND DESERTIFICATION

# Introduction

Today, deforestation and desertification are critical environmental issues, causing widespread harm globally. Tropical rainforests are vanishing, while drylands in arid regions are degrading rapidly. These processes diminish land's ability to sustain life and disrupt ecosystems worldwide.

Human activities and climate change drive deforestation and desertification. Industrialisation and urbanisation in developed countries historically caused significant environmental destruction, leading to shortages of essential resources like plants, animals, food, and water, along with medicines and fuel.

Addressing these challenges is crucial for global economic growth. It requires concerted efforts from all nations to mitigate them and safeguard the environment for future generations.

# Forests

**Forests are vital for sustaining global ecosystems, supporting plants, animals, and humans alike. They occupy 31% of the earth's land surface and host 80% of terrestrial plant species. However, deforestation poses a grave threat, leading to the extinction risk of many plant and animal species.**

## Types of Forests

There are 3 main types of forests:

- Deciduous forests thrive in regions with mild winters and humid, wet summers, found in Asia, Europe, Australia, New Zealand, North America, and South America.
- Coniferous forests flourish in areas with long, cold winters and cool, short summers, mainly found in East Asia, Canada, Europe, North America, and South America.
- Rainforests, housing nearly 50% of the world's plant and animal species, grow in regions with heavy rainfall and consistent sunlight, predominantly found in parts of Africa, Southeast Asia, and South and Central America.

**FUN FACT**

Around 30 million species of plants and animals are found in tropical rainforests.

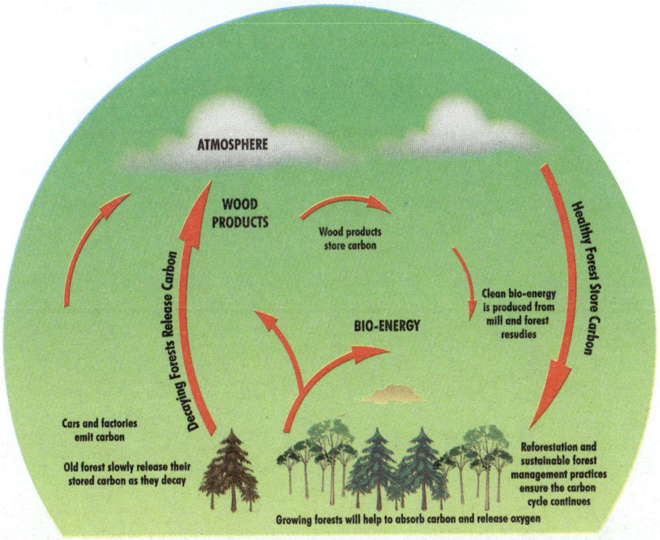


? Carbon dioxide is a greenhouse gas. (True or False)

## The Forest Cycle

Forests undergo growth and death cycles, absorbing and releasing carbon, acting as a carbon sink. Carbon dioxide, a greenhouse gas, traps heat from the sun, raising global temperatures. Tropical deforestation contributes to approximately 20% of annual carbon dioxide emissions globally. Increasing temperatures lead to natural disasters, highlighting the importance of forest plantation to mitigate the effects of global warming.

# Deforestation

**Deforestation involves clearing plants and trees to repurpose land. Global deforestation commenced in 1960, and by the late 19th century, many of the world's dense forests had been cleared. Since then, deforestation rates have escalated significantly.**

## History

About 300 million years ago, the Carboniferous rainforests faced destruction due to climate change, resulting in the extinction of numerous plant and animal species. Since then, rainforests have steadily diminished in size.

## Global Deforestation

Rapid population growth and poverty have driven increased demand for farming, cattle grazing, commodity plantation, urbanisation, and industrial growth. These activities are major contributors to global deforestation.

## Growing Urbanisation

Nearly 90-95% of rainforests along Brazil's Atlantic coast have been cleared, posing significant risks to the global climate and environment.

? Which country has the highest rate of deforestation? ________________

**FUN FACT**

The FAO reports that Nigeria holds the record for the highest deforestation rate of primary forests worldwide.

# Causes of Deforestation

**For millennia, humans have cleared land for farming and raising livestock. With the rise of civilisations, urbanisation and industrialisation increased, leading to land clearance for purposes beyond agriculture, including construction of roads, industries, and cities.**

### Development of Infrastructure

Human civilisation has advanced significantly since the era of hunter-gatherers, but our progress has caused considerable harm to the planet. Daily, millions worldwide travel between places using trains, buses, and cars. Ever considered how much land has been cleared to create these connections?

### Food Requirements

To meet food demands, vast forested areas worldwide are converted to agricultural land and pastures. Migratory farmers often clear land by burning trees. Besides crops, land is cleared for livestock, driven by global meat demand. In Brazil, cattle grazing alone causes about 80% of rainforest destruction.

### Subsistence farming

Poverty is often cited as a key factor in deforestation. In numerous regions globally, farmers engage in subsistence farming, which involves cultivating food crops to fulfil the needs of their own families.

**FUN FACT**

**By 2018, humans had reduced forest area by around 30% and grasslands/shrubs by about 68%, mainly to accommodate livestock grazing and crop cultivation for human consumption.**

**?** In Brazil, cattle grazing is responsible for about ______ of rainforest destruction.

# Lumber Industry

Since the Industrial Revolution, the demand for timber has risen sharply. Initially, coal mining started in the seventeenth century, but timber remained a key fuel source for many industries. Today, many industries still use wood for energy production, with most logged trees serving this purpose.

## Paper Production

Wood pulp is used in paper production. Every year, major paper producers worldwide cut down forests, with nearly 35% of trees felled for this purpose. However, in recent years, there has been a move towards sustainable practices, including paper recycling.

## Furniture and Construction

Timber is also essential in building construction and flooring. Thousands of acres of tropical forests are cleared annually to meet these demands.

## Illegal Logging

Most tree logging worldwide is illegal due to weak enforcement of laws by governments and corporate greed, which has fostered the growth of illegal timber gangs. The Congo Basin in Africa and the Amazon rainforests face the most serious threats from illegal logging.

**FUN FACT**

The United States is the world's largest producer and consumer of timber.

? Timber is used in flooring. (True/False)

# Climate Change & Forests

Forests play a crucial role in maintaining the balance of the water cycle. Disrupting the Earth's water cycle contributes to climate change, impacting food production, water supplies, human health, and overall well-being.

### Water Cycle

Deforestation disrupts the water recycling process within forest ecosystems, resulting in decreased precipitation and drier climates. Reduced rainfall levels can impact essential human needs like access to drinking water and irrigation. Additionally, this could potentially lead to the extinction of certain species.

### Irregular Rainfall

Although deforestation primarily affects precipitation in and around the cleared regions, it also influences rainfall in mid and high latitudes. For instance, deforestation in the Amazon affects rainfall from Mexico to Texas, and deforestation in Southeast Asia changes rainfall patterns in China and the Balkan Peninsula.

### Warming of Earth

Forests shield the ground from direct sunlight. When trees are removed, the exposed earth warms up, heating the air above and leading to drier climates and global temperature increases, contributing to shifts in climate patterns.

**FUN FACT**

Around 125,000 years ago, the sea level was 8 meters higher than it is today.

**?** Disturbing the earth's ____________ leads to climate change.

# Biodiversity Disaster

Biodiversity encompasses the various species and life forms found on Earth, contributing to human health and well-being. Deforestation disrupts ecosystems, ultimately resulting in the loss of biodiversity.

### Loss of Rainforest Species

Rainforests are vital for global biodiversity, with 25% of modern medicines derived from their plants. Around 80% of plant and animal species inhabit these areas. Deforestation here leads to an estimated loss of 50,000 species annually.

### Disappearing Animals

Tree removal devastates forest habitats and food sources, posing a threat to various species like the African elephant. In the early 20th century, there may have been 3-5 million African elephants, but today, their population has dwindled to around 415,000.

### Mass Extinctions

A recent study suggests that by the end of the 21st century, over 40% of plant and animal species in Southeast Asia could confront mass extinction. Additionally, up to 75% of the earth's reef-building corals are at risk of extinction. If global temperatures rise by 3.5°C, as many as 70% of well-known species could face extinction.

**FUN FACT**

Tropical rainforests experience the highest rate of species extinction.

? Does biodiversity contribute to the health and well-being of humans?

# Deforestation in China

In the mid-1990s, China emerged as one of the world's top timber exporters. Today, deforestation poses a significant challenge in China, primarily driven by commercial logging.

### Ban on Logging

In the last two decades, about 50% of forests in northern and central China have been deforested to meet wood and timber demands. In 1999, the Chinese government banned forest logging and imposed a tax on wooden flooring, resulting in increased wood imports. This demand was met through illegal logging and deforestation in other countries such as Siberia, Brazil, and Indonesia.

### The Great Green Wall

Chinese citizens and the government are actively engaged in reforestation efforts. Initiated in 1978, the Great Green Wall project mandates every citizen above the age of 11 to plant at least three saplings annually. In the past decade, Chinese citizens have collectively planted approximately 56 billion trees nationwide.

### Illegal Logging on the Rise

The increasing demand for wood in China has spurred illegal logging in several countries, including Madagascar, Indonesia, and the Philippines. Large quantities of illegal tropical rainforest timber from Indonesia, rosewood from Madagascar, and tree trunks from the Philippines were exported to China.

**FUN FACT**

21.9% of the total Chinese land is covered with forests.

? Is deforestation a major issue in China? ____________________

# Palm Oil Cultivation

Palm oil plantations have grown rapidly in recent years, touted as an eco-friendly fuel and a cost-effective alternative to other vegetable oils. It's also considered a healthier food choice and easy to produce. Malaysia and Indonesia account for about 87% of global palm oil production.

### Environmental Impact

In the past two decades, Southeast Asia's rainforests have been swiftly cleared for palm oil cultivation, causing global warming, drought, landslides, pollution, desertification, soil nutrient loss, and biodiversity decline. Palm oil cultivation is a major factor in the region's deforestation, with around two million square meters destroyed every hour through burning.

### Impact on Biodiversity

These rainforests are home to around 20,000 flowering plant species, 3,000 tree species, 300,000 animal species, and many other unknown species. There are only around 60,000 orangutans left on the Indonesian islands of Sumatra and Borneo.

**FUN FACT**

Palm oil cultivation poses a threat to both local and global environments in Southeast Asia.

### Impact on Human Life

Palm oil cultivation is also harming the physical well-being and livelihoods of local inhabitants in Southeast Asia. In 2011, a landslide in Thailand claimed the lives of around 40 people, with researchers linking the incident to palm oil cultivation in the area.

? What percentage of the world's palm oil is produced by Malaysia and Indonesia? _____

# Amazon Rainforests

The Amazon rainforest, often called the 'Lungs of our Planet', is the world's largest tropical rainforest, spanning 1.4 billion acres of land and generating nearly 20%of the world's oxygen. It encompasses about half of Brazil and significant areas in Colombia, Venezuela, and the eastern regions of Peru.

### Deforestation

About 47% of the Amazon rainforest has been deforested. Since the 1990s, deforestation in the Amazon has steadily increased each year. Compared to 1992, deforestation rose by 32% in 1996 and by 18% from 2000 to 2005 compared to the previous five years.

### Effects

The exploitation of the Amazon rainforest has severely affected the lives of local people. Since the 1990s, over 90 tribes have been destroyed, leaving just 200,000 individuals out of a population of 10 million in Amazonia, from 500 years ago. Forest removal also contributes to greenhouse gas emissions, biodiversity loss, global warming, CO2 release into the atmosphere, water and air pollution, flooding, and soil erosion.

### Causes

Deforestation in the Amazon is caused by cattle grazing, large-scale soybean farming, and property construction, with cattle ranching accounting for 60-70% of the deforestation.

**FUN FACT**

The Amazon rainforest covers enough area to create a new country.

? Almost ____________ percent of the Amazon rainforest has been deforested.

# Deforestation in Madagascar

**Madagascar, the world's fourth largest island, is also one of the poorest countries. Since humans arrived about 2,000 years ago, over 90% of the original forests have been destroyed. The onset of French rule in 1895 hastened this destruction, with almost 70% of the forest cover lost.**

*A satellite map of Madagascar. The brown areas depict deforested land.*

### Effects

Massive deforestation in Madagascar has resulted in the island's inability to produce and supply enough food, shelter, fresh water, and sanitation facilities to its expanding population. This deforestation has also caused global warming, diminished biodiversity, soil erosion, and desertification in the area.

### Soil erosion

Due to extensive deforestation, many areas in Madagascar suffer from soil erosion. The removal of trees leads to the erosion of nutrient-rich topsoil, leaving much of the land infertile. About 400 tonnes of soil per 10,000 sq m are lost to erosion annually, polluting the nearby Indian Ocean.

### Animal Extinction

The destruction of Madagascar's forests has endangered numerous species, including insects, tortoises, giant predatory raptors, giant lemurs, and hippopotamuses. At least 17 species of giant lemurs and nearly all large animal species have become extinct. The silky sifaka, one of the rarest mammals, inhabits Madagascar's forests and is on the brink of extinction due to deforestation.

**FUN FACT**

The introduction of coffee as a cash crop during the French rule is a significant cause of deforestation in Madagascar.

? Since 1895, almost half of the forests of Madagascar have been deforested. (True or False)

# Desertification

**Desertification refers to the degradation of land in drylands, where the soil becomes dry and incapable of supporting vegetation. It is a rapid process that can transform drylands into deserts within a few seasons.**

## Drylands

Drylands, characterized by little and irregular rainfall throughout the year, face challenges with water availability. Desertification impacts the livelihoods of millions of people who rely on these areas for farming and other activities.

## Coverage

Drylands affected by desertification are primarily found in arid, semi-arid, and sub-humid regions worldwide, covering up to 40% of the Earth's land surface. Around 50% of countries globally have parts or all of their lands in dryland environments. Approximately 25% of the world's land has already been impacted by desertification.

## Danger to Crop Cultivation

Drylands are rich in biodiversity and crucial for food production, growing vital grains like maize, wheat, rice, and millet. Over 30% of global crops come from drylands. However, 10-20% of these areas have already been destroyed, endangering over a billion people from future desertification.

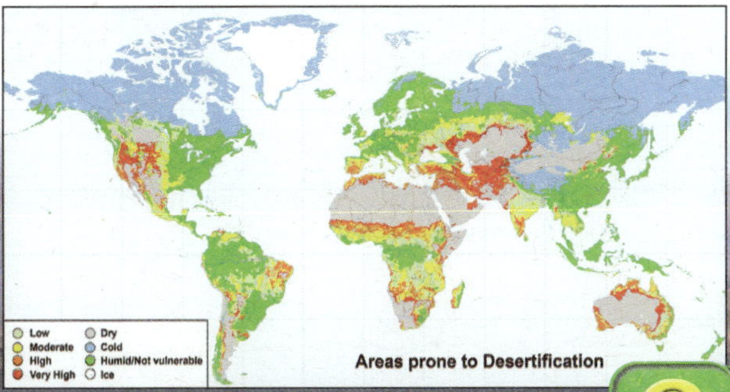

Areas prone to Desertification

**FUN FACT**

Drylands in approximately 110 countries are at risk of desertification.

**?** About half of the world's land has already been affected by desertification. (True or False)

# Causes of Desertification-I

Human activities like over-cultivation, poor farming, irrigation techniques, and overgrazing have reduced drylands' productivity, leading to climate change, global warming, and the greenhouse effect. This interaction between the environment and human actions promotes desertification.

### Over Cultivation

The rapidly growing population is one of the factors driving farmers to over cultivate land. Continuous cultivation of crops on the same land for years diminishes soil fertility and productivity. This harms soil structure, eventually leading to desertification of the over-cultivated land.

### Overgrazing

Historically, humans moved livestock based on food and water availability, but settlement in areas with stable food sources limited mobility. Continuous grazing on the same land by livestock has worsened desertification.

### Poor Farming Methods

Monoculture, intensive agriculture, canal irrigation, and pesticide use hinder plant growth and contribute to desertification. In 2010, a severe drought in the Sahel region placed millions at risk of starvation. The drought resulted mainly from overcultivation, overgrazing, and inadequate farming and irrigation practices.

**FUN FACT**

Each year, approximately 5 million tonnes of pesticides are used globally for agricultural purposes.

? Desertification encourages overgrazing and over cultivation of land. (True or False)

# Causes of Desertification-II

Desertification stems from both natural causes and human activities. Natural factors like climate changes and disasters such as droughts, hurricanes, and floods contribute to it. These causes can vary over time or location but ultimately lead to decreased land productivity and degradation.

### Climate Change

Human activities, like burning fossil fuels, have increased greenhouse gas levels in the atmosphere. Over the past 100 years, this has raised global temperatures by 0.3°C to 0.6°C, leading to significant climate changes. Altered rainfall patterns in many areas cause damaging droughts, floods, and desertification.

### Droughts

Drought is a prolonged dry weather period caused by insufficient rainfall in an area. The threat of drought can trigger human activities like overgrazing and overcultivation. From 1960 to 1980, the Sahel region endured a severe drought, resulting in nearly 100,000 deaths.

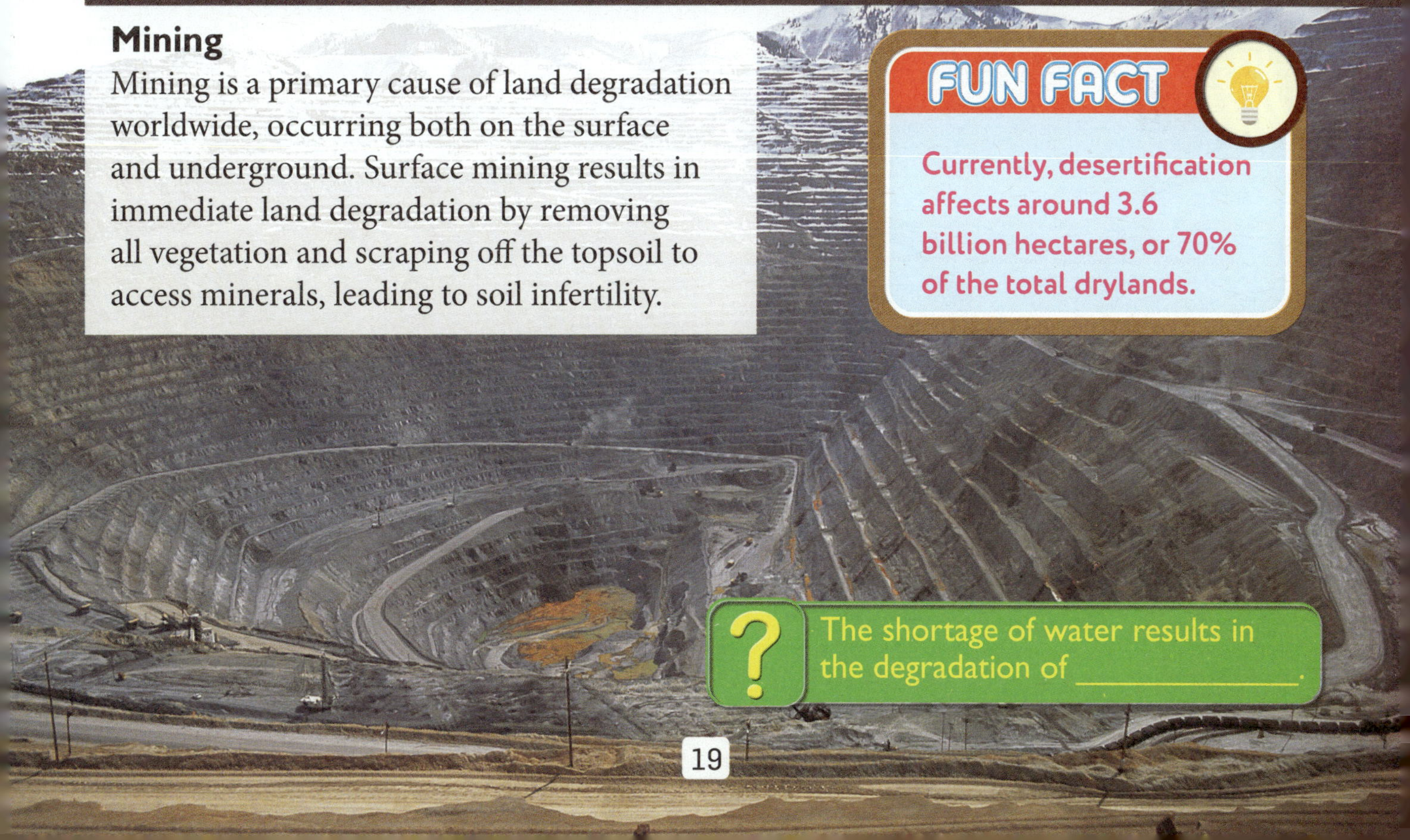

### Mining

Mining is a primary cause of land degradation worldwide, occurring both on the surface and underground. Surface mining results in immediate land degradation by removing all vegetation and scraping off the topsoil to access minerals, leading to soil infertility.

**FUN FACT**

Currently, desertification affects around 3.6 billion hectares, or 70% of the total drylands.

**?** The shortage of water results in the degradation of ______________.

# Impact of Desertification

Desertification has adverse environmental, social, and physical impacts, reducing the land's capacity to support life. This directly affects plants, livestock, agricultural crops, people, and the development of countries worldwide.

### Environmental Impact

Desertification dries and impoverishes soil, making it unable to sustain plant and animal life. This degradation significantly impacts the water cycle and the environment, causing soil erosion, water erosion, landslides, droughts, dust storms, soil acidification, pollution, and increased salinity.

### Social Impact

Desertification and land degradation force rural populations to abandon farming and migrate to urban areas for new opportunities. In just over 20 years, approximately 10 million people in Africa have migrated to cities seeking a better life.

### Physical Impact

Desertification impacts around 1.2 billion people globally, leading to poverty, vegetation loss, and emigration. Currently, in the Sahel region, over 18 million people face hunger, with approximately 1 million children at risk of malnutrition.

**FUN FACT**

Every year, approximately 12 million hectares of land become useless due to desertification.

? Around ____________ people worldwide are affected because of desertification.

# Ecosystem and Biodiversity

An ecosystem encompasses the plants and animals in a specific area that depend on each other and their surroundings. Therefore, if any element of the ecosystem is affected, the entire ecosystem is likely to suffer.

**Damaged Ecosystems**

Animals and plant species in drylands are highly adapted to their extreme environment. However, drought, land overexploitation, and salinity destroy soil, habitats, and food and water sources.

**Plant Biodiversity**

Desertification has diminished approximately 12.5% of the world's plant biodiversity. This reduction in plant biodiversity contributes to changing climates, global warming, and the loss of habitats and animal species.

**Animal Biodiversity**

Animals lacking food, shelter, and protection face a heightened risk of extinction. In Spain during the 20th century, urbanization and poor farming practices destroyed the habitat of the Iberian lynx, reducing their population to just 100 individuals.

**FUN FACT**

According to the International Union for Conservation of Nature (IUCN), over 44,000 species are threatened with extinction.

? Are human beings and animals dependent on plants? ____________________

# Desertification in China

Desertification is a significant environmental challenge in China, with approximately 28% of the total area either enclosed by desert or experiencing desertification. Over 70% of land degradation occurs in the northern, northwestern, and northeastern regions of China.

### Human Contribution

The rapid population growth has resulted in the over utilisation of land resources, including intensified agricultural activities and animal husbandry. Additionally, mining, tourism, and urban development have also led to land degradation in China.

### Dust Storms

Extreme droughts have had significant environmental impacts in Beijing, China's capital. Strong winds frequently transport soil from the drylands of Northwest China hundreds of miles to the eastern regions, creating massive dust clouds. Over the past two decades, dust storms have become an annual occurrence in Beijing.

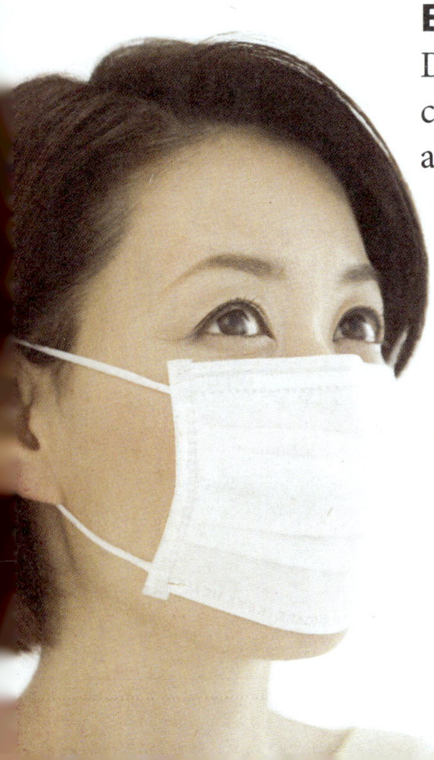

### Effects of Dust Clouds

Dust clouds are thick and choking, causing breathing difficulties, asthma attacks, and allergic reactions. During windy spring days, people often wear masks due to reduced visibility on roads, slowing down traffic. Flights may be cancelled, and airports closed as a safety precaution.

**FUN FACT**

Desertification has affected around 400 million people in China in recent decades.

**?** Which part of China faces severe land degradation? ____________________

# Desertification in Africa

Desertification has had the most significant impact in Africa, where two-thirds of the land is covered by deserts and drylands, with 27% already degraded. In recent years, the rate of food production and crop yields in many parts of Africa has rapidly declined.

### South Africa

Roughly 50% of Southern Africa is comprised of semi-arid land, which, due to human activities, has developed desert-like conditions. Presently, approximately 30% of South African land is severely degraded, while the remaining portion is at risk of desertification.

### Impact on Human Life

Since 2001, consecutive droughts in South Africa have posed serious threats to the livelihoods of millions. In 2002-03, a food deficit of approximately 3.3 million tonnes affected nearly 14.4 million people. The degraded land is no longer viable for crop production or livestock grazing.

### Lake Chad

Over the last 40 years, Lake Chad, one of Africa's largest freshwater lakes, has shrunk to just one-twelfth of its original size. Once spanning 25,000 sq km in 1963, it has since shrunk by 95%. Researchers attribute this decline to human activities and warn that without intervention, the lake could completely evaporate within the next 20 years.

**FUN FACT**

Farm yields across Africa are only one-thirds of those achieved by their Asian counterparts.

? What percentage of the South African land is severely degraded? ____________

# Sustainable Practices

**Our planet is struggling to withstand human demands. It's crucial for people and nations to come together and address this global threat. Adopting sustainable forestry practices is essential to preserve our forests and tackle the challenges posed by climate change.**

## Sustainable Forestry

Unsustainable practices in the Amazon rainforest have degraded over one-third of its forestry land. To address this issue, sustainable agricultural methods should be implemented. Farmers should adopt practices like agroforestry (cultivating trees alongside crops) and intercropping.

## How can I contribute?

We can all help save the planet by reducing paper consumption, minimizing waste, opting for paperless billing, and recycling paper whenever possible. Choose products from sustainable manufacturers and prioritise those with reliable eco-friendly logos. Additionally, contribute to tree planting and learn how to care for plants and soil.

## Reforestation

Governments and citizens must work together to increase global forested areas. China's reforestation efforts have raised its forest cover from 12% to 16.55% over the last two decades. Similarly, many East Asian countries have expanded their forests through reforestation and afforestation initiatives, adding approximately 1 million hectares of forestry land from 2000 to 2005.

**FUN FACT**

World Forestry Day is celebrated on March 21st.

? When is World Forestry Day celebrated? ______________

# Glossary

**Biofuel:** fuel derived from biomass.

**Canal irrigation:** waterway transporting water from a source to soil.

**Combat:** fight against something.

**Combustion:** rapid oxidation with heat and light.

**Commodity:** trade and exchange article.

**Constraint:** limitation or restriction.

**Degradation:** deterioration.

**Devastating:** highly destructive.

**Endangered:** threatened with danger.

**Exploitation:** selfish utilization.

**Extinction:** dying out.

**Grazing:** feeding on grassland.

**Greenhouse effect:** atmospheric heating.

**Indigenous:** native.

**Infertile:** unproductive.

**Inhabitant:** permanent resident.

**Landslide:** downward soil sliding.

**Livelihood:** means of support.

**Monoculture:** single-crop land use.

**Offsetting:** counteracting.

**Pasture:** grazing land.

**Pesticide:** plant pest chemical.

**Plantation:** planted trees or plants.

**Progressively:** changing in stages.

**Ranching:** livestock raising.

**Retreating:** moving back or withdrawing.

**Sanitation:** health and cleanliness protection.

**Scarcity:** insufficient supply.

**Shielding:** protection.

**Starvation:** state of extreme hunger.

**Sustainable:** maintained at a certain rate or level.

**Timber:** prepared wood for building.

**Topsoil:** upper part of the soil.

**Vegetation:** all area plants as a whole.

**Yielding:** productive.

## Answers

Page 7 - True
Page 8 - Nigeria
Page 9 - 90%
Page 10 - True
Page 11 - Water cycle
Page 12 - Yes
Page 13 - Yes
Page 14 - 87%
Page 15 - 47
Page 16 - False
Page 17 - False
Page 18 - False
Page 19 - Natural vegetation
Page 20 - 1.2 billion
Page 21 - Yes
Page 22 - Northern
Page 23 - 30%
Page 24 - 21 March

# SAVE WATER

# Introduction

Water is vital for both humans and animals, making its conservation imperative. Global warming has altered weather patterns, impacting water quantity and quality. Pollution, population growth, and urbanisation further strain freshwater resources.

Treating polluted water consumes substantial energy. Efficient water use not only conserves energy but also averts future water crises when demand surpasses supply.

# Importance of Water

**Only a small fraction of Earth's water is suitable for drinking, agriculture, industry, and domestic use. Freshwater consumption has surged tenfold since 1900, while its availability diminishes due to global warming. Failing to conserve water now may precipitate a severe future water crisis.**

### Current Condition

Currently, over 1.3 billion individuals reside in regions with a physical water scarcity, while approximately 1.6 billion face economic water shortages, hindering efficient water extraction. Sub-Saharan Africa is particularly affected. Projections suggest that by 2025, around 1.8 billion people will inhabit water-scarce areas.

**FUN FACT**

On an average, an Australian consumes almost 1 million litres of fresh water annually.

### Crisis, Stress and Scarcity

When an area's water demand surpasses its availability, it signals a water crisis. Despite Earth having sufficient freshwater to meet global needs, many regions currently face water crises due to uneven distribution, wastage, pollution, and global warming. Water stress occurs when annual supply drops below 1,700 m3 per person, while water scarcity is defined as supply falling below 1,000 m3 per person.

? When an area's water demand is more than the available water, it indicates a ________.

# Freshwater Resources

**The Earth, often called the 'blue planet,' is mostly covered by water, making up 75% of its surface. However, only about 3% of this water is freshwater, with the rest being salty. The distribution of the freshwater is uneven globally.**

## Groundwater

Roughly 30% of Earth's freshwater exists deep underground, within layers of rock and soil known as aquifers. These aquifers are replenished by surface water seepage. Groundwater, primarily accessed through handpumps, motor pumps, and wells, serves as a clean source of drinking water. However, its quality is increasingly threatened by global warming.

## Surface Water

Surface water, including lakes, rivers, and freshwater wetlands, accounts for just 0.9% of total freshwater resources. Despite being renewable sources replenished by rainfall and snowfall, they are facing challenges such as over-extraction, pollution, and climate change, leading to a decline in their quantity.

**FUN FACT**

Brazil has the largest supply of fresh water.

**?** What percentage of global water is salty? __________

# Water Stressors

**Many countries, despite having adequate freshwater sources, face water scarcity due to various stressors. To mitigate this, careful water usage and effective management of stressors are essential.**

## Major Water Stressors

Overpopulation, particularly in developing nations, exacerbates the strain on water resources. Predictions suggest a global population increase of about 3 billion by 2050, with 90% of this growth expected in developing countries. Migration to regions with abundant water exacerbates water stress, with over 191 million migrants worldwide. Additionally, changes in precipitation patterns due to global warming further compound water stress.

## Economic Development

With rapid global economic development, water consumption is on the rise, driven largely by industries such as business, tourism, and entertainment. These sectors contribute significantly to the use of virtual water, which is water embedded in finished products or used during production.

? The increasing population puts stress on water resources. (True/False)

**FUN FACT**

Groundwater in many European cities with populations exceeding 100,000 is being depleted at a faster rate than it can be replenished.

# Global Warming

**Rising global temperatures are increasing the demand for freshwater, putting stress on its availability. Both the quantity and quality of water are deteriorating rapidly, signaling a future water crisis. To prevent a shortage of fresh water, efforts to combat global warming must be intensified.**

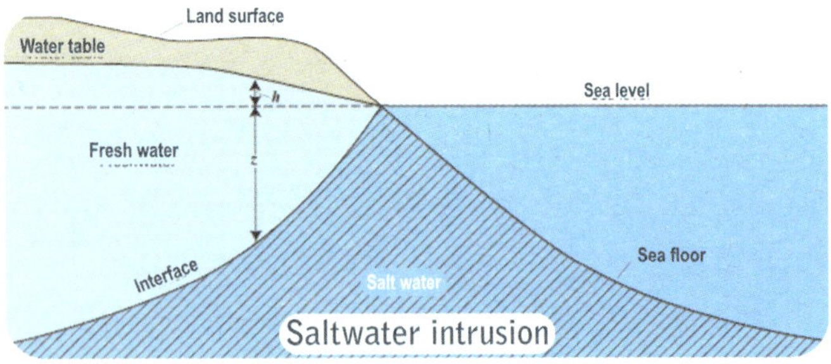


## Increasing Salinity

Rising sea levels, driven by excess warming and glacial melting, are causing saline water to infiltrate surface waters and aquifers along the Gulf, Pacific, and Atlantic coasts. This intrusion is deteriorating freshwater quality, posing health risks to coastal populations.

**FUN FACT**

Since the 1890s, sea levels have risen by an average of 6 to 9 inches.

## Water Levels of Lakes

Rising temperatures are leading to decreased precipitation in some regions and increased evapotranspiration, resulting in declining water levels in lakes. Scientists predict that Lake Huron and Lake Michigan in central North America will decrease by about 4.5 ft in the next century.

## Effect on Groundwater

Increasing evapotranspiration and frequent droughts are causing aquifer water levels to plummet in many countries. Conversely, in regions experiencing more rainfall and floods, aquifers aren't replenishing properly because much of the water is drained away rather than percolating through the soil.

? Global warming is causing saline water to intrude into fresh water. (True/False)

# Water for Agriculture

**Agriculture is responsible for approximately 70% of global fresh water withdrawals from lakes, aquifers, and rivers. The decline in fresh water resources significantly impacts global food production. To maintain stable food production and prices, water conservation and management are essential.**

## Rain-fed Agriculture

Rain-fed agriculture relies solely on rainwater for irrigation, known as green water. It's a widespread practice globally, especially for major crops like wheat, rice, and maize. Approximately 80% of the world's cultivated land depends on rainwater, contributing to 60% of total crop production.

### FUN FACT

Rain-fed agriculture prevails across significant regions: about 90% in Latin America, 95% in sub-Saharan Africa, and 65% in East Asia.

## Irrigated Agriculture

In this agriculture type, water for crop production is sourced from surface and ground waters, known as blue water. While only 20% of global cultivated land relies on blue water irrigation, it competes significantly with other sectors for fresh water. Regions like the Great Plains, North China Plain, and Punjab may face crop production losses if water withdrawals remain unchecked.

## Water Loss in Irrigation

Despite challenges in irrigation system management and failures in some regions, there's a rising demand for increased irrigation. However, the focus should be on efficient water use. Currently, 60% of irrigation water is lost to seepage and evaporation before reaching crops.

? What percentage of the world's cultivated land depends on rainwater? ____________

# Industrial Uses

**Industries, recreation, and other sectors also rely heavily on fresh water. With global warming impacting water quantity and quality, these industries are compelled to develop water recycling and conservation strategies to safeguard their future operations.**

### Industrial Sector

About 22% of the world's fresh water is used by industries, including power plants, refineries, and manufacturing. However, their wastewater discharge contributes to pollution. Governments have enforced regulations to ensure proper treatment of industrial wastewater before it's returned to the environment.

### Thermal Power Plants

Thermal power plants are major water consumers globally, using steam-driven turbine generators to produce electricity. This process requires significant water for equipment cooling, but the heated water cannot be returned to the environment.

### Recreational Sector

Water is utilised in recreational pursuits like sailing, water skiing, swimming, diving, surfing, and golf. While golf requires significant water for maintaining green grounds, the other activities do not consume water. Nevertheless, their use of freshwater restricts its availability for more critical sectors like agriculture and industry.

**FUN FACT**

About 1,850 gallons of fresh water is needed to refine one barrel of oil.

? Which sector is the biggest user of fresh water after agriculture? ____________

# Efficient Irrigation

**In the past four decades, many countries have adopted improved crop varieties and water-efficient irrigation methods, resulting in nearly doubled crop yields. For instance, in 2005, Europe achieved cereal production of five tonnes per hectare through such practices.**

### Deficit Irrigation (DI)

Farmers worldwide are preparing for the looming water crisis by adopting deficit irrigation methods. These techniques involve providing crops with less water than they require, inducing a slight stress that promotes drought tolerance. Crops like cotton, maize, groundnut, wheat, and sugar beet, less sensitive to water stress, can adapt well to these practices, leading to significant water savings with minimal impact on overall crop production.

### Drip Irrigation

Drip irrigation, also known as trickle irrigation, is a modern farming method used in water-scarce areas. It delivers water slowly to plant roots, drop by drop, through pipes with valves and drippers. This method is popular for growing various crops like bananas, coconuts, tomatoes, grapes, strawberries, maize, cotton, and sugarcane. In India, it's widely used in regions such as the horticulture belt of West Maharashtra and the cotton belt of Khandesh and Marathwada.

**FUN FACT**

About 84% of water withdrawals in Asia are allocated for agricultural purposes.

**?** Which irrigation method supplies water drop by drop to crops? ______________

# Gardens and Lawns

**A significant portion of household fresh water is dedicated to irrigating landscapes, gardens, and lawns. Contrary to common belief, maintaining lush gardens doesn't necessarily require excessive watering and fertilisation. Implementing water-efficient lawn care practices can significantly conserve water.**

## Water Carefully

Manual watering is more efficient for lawn irrigation, saving about 34% of water compared to systems like in-ground sprinklers that release water automatically at a fixed time. Adding rain and soil moisture sensors to automatic systems improves efficiency by preventing irrigation during rain or when soil moisture is sufficient.

## Minimize Turf Grass

Areas covered with grass are known as turf grass regions and often require substantial water for maintenance. To conserve water, consider using grass varieties like Turffalo grass that require less water. Additionally, limit turf grass to areas like playgrounds rather than covering the entire property.

## Choose Plants Wisely

Choose native plants for your garden as they adapt well to the local climate, soil, and sunlight. They require minimal water and fertilisers and are resistant to insects and pests. Opting for these plants can help conserve water and contribute to environmental sustainability.

? ____________ releases water automatically at a fixed time.

**FUN FACT**

Lawns require a maximum of 25 mm/1 inch of water per week for maintenance.

# Rainwater Harvesting

**Rainwater harvesting is among the most cost-effective methods for water conservation. It helps prevent contamination of fresh water and alleviates pressure on groundwater supplies. By utilising rainwater for non-agricultural purposes, such as domestic use, it reduces the strain on both surface and groundwater resources.**

## Storage for Future

During summer water shortages, rainwater can be efficiently utilized for tasks like car washing, house cleaning, and filling swimming pools. Installing rain barrels, which collect rainwater from rooftops, is an effective method. These barrels feature sieves to filter out debris and insects, saving over 1,300 gallons of fresh water in a typical household. Similarly, the recreation sector can also benefit from rainwater harvesting techniques.

## Immediate Use of Rainwater

Rain gardens capture rainwater from rooftops and driveways for garden irrigation, preventing runoff and filtering more water into the ground than regular lawns. Gravel or porous pavements also help by allowing rainwater to permeate the soil, recharging aquifers.

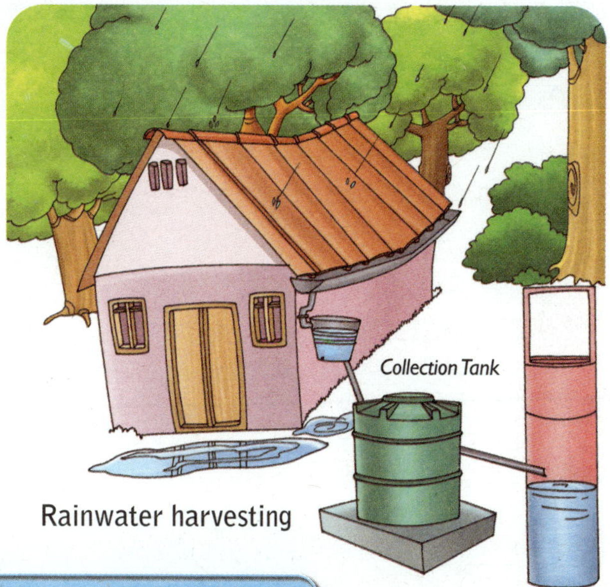


Rainwater harvesting

**FUN FACT**

At present, Brazil and China have the biggest rainwater harvesting systems.

? Rainwater harvesting helps in conserving fresh water. (True/False)

# Recycled Water

**Recycled water, also known as treated wastewater or sewage, undergoes treatment in water treatment plants to remove contaminants. It is then sold at lower rates to encourage its usage. While popular in developed nations, in developing ones, about 80% of sewage is discharged untreated into rivers.**

## Non-potable Uses

About 36% of reclaimed water globally is used in agriculture, supplying vital nutrients for crops like wheat and maize. It's also used for irrigating lawns, golf courses, and municipal tasks such as firefighting and street cleaning in the US and the UK.

## Recharging Groundwater

Recycled water, although not safe for direct consumption, can augment potable water supplies indirectly. Injected into aquifers, it undergoes treatment before being extracted, rendering it suitable for drinking. This method, termed groundwater recharging, often involves constructing lateral shafts with bore wells.

**FUN FACT**

In Singapore, the reclaimed water produced by the Public Utilities Board is called NEWater.

? What is the other name for reclaimed water? ______________________

# Recycling Grey Water

**Grey water, generated from domestic activities like dishwashing, bathing, and laundering, can be treated and recycled for flushing toilets and irrigating lawns. Unlike grey water, black water from toilets containing feces and urine cannot be recycled.**

### Benefits

The use of recycled grey water helps reduce the usage of fresh water for purposes other than drinking and cooking. This, in turn, decreases the excessive discharge of waste water into treatment plants, leading to more effective and efficient treatment. Additionally, excess grey water used to water plants helps recharge groundwater as it seeps into the soil.

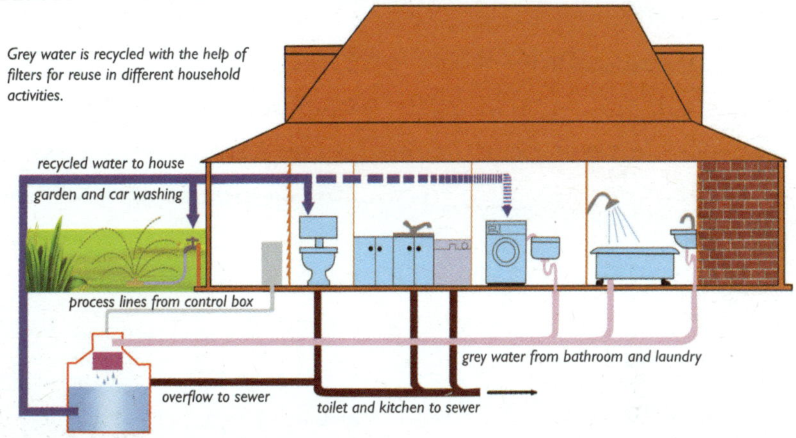


### Treating Grey Water

During grey water treatment, solid pollutants are removed by passing the water through a filter. Chlorine bleach is then added to disinfect it. Afterward, the water is left undisturbed to allow solid contaminants to settle down and any fats and oils to emerge on the surface, leaving treated grey water in the middle.

### Proper Usage

Grey water contains dissolved soaps and detergents, which can have harmful effects on the growth of plants if used without treatment for irrigating gardens. It is advisable to use treated grey water for flushing toilets, as untreated grey water may leave stains and produce a foul smell after a few hours.

**FUN FACT**

After 24 hours, stored grey water becomes as harmful as black water.

? Black water can be recycled and used for irrigating lawns. (True/False)

# Desalination

**Desalination is the process of removing salt from water, making it suitable for drinking. This helps preserve groundwater for essential purposes, as other freshwater needs can be fulfilled with desalinated water. Countries like Israel and Saudi Arabia, facing chronic freshwater shortages, have invested in desalination plants to address their water needs.**

### Distillation

In desalination, saline water is heated in tanks and the steam produced is condensed to obtain fresh water. Heat from the steam in one tank is used to heat water in the next tank, minimising energy consumption. The Minjur Desalination Plant in Chennai, India, is the largest in South Asia, producing 36.5 million cubic meters of fresh water annually.

### Multiple-effect Distillation

In this process, pure water from heating salty water flows into the next chamber, where it's boiled again by the heat energy it carries, producing more vapour. However, this technique is suitable only for small-scale desalination.

A desalination plant

### Reverse Osmosis

Reverse osmosis is a widely used desalination process. Salty water is placed on one side of a tank divided by a semipermeable membrane, while clean water is obtained on the other side. Pressure forces fresh water to flow out, leaving salt behind. This method purifies water up to 98%. In Perth, Australia, 17% of potable water comes from seawater using this process.

**FUN FACT**

The Jebel Ali Desalination Plant in the United Arab Emirates is the world's largest.

Name the two methods of desalination.
1. ____________ 2. ____________

# Seawater Greenhouse

**In 1991, British inventor Charlie Paton developed seawater greenhouse technology to address the lack of freshwater for agriculture in arid regions. This method harnesses solar energy to desalinate seawater, providing a sustainable solution for crop cultivation.**

## How it Works

Seawater greenhouse technology operates in several stages. Firstly, seawater is pumped into the evaporator's first wall. As air flows through, it's filtered from dust and pollen, becoming cool and humid. Next, only beneficial sunlight for photosynthesis enters, filtered through the roof, ensuring a cool environment while providing sufficient sunlight for crop growth. Humidified air then moves to a second evaporator, reaching saturation. It then passes through a condenser, cooled by cold seawater pipes, causing distilled water to condense and be collected for irrigation.

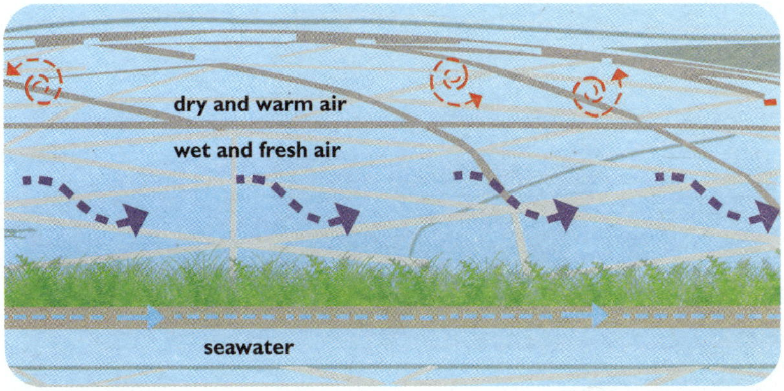


## Benefits

Seawater greenhouse technology relies solely on solar energy, eliminating the need for fossil fuels. It operates at a 10 to 20% lower cost than conventional greenhouses by generating its own electricity and utilising seawater nutrients for crop fertilisation.

**FUN FACT**

The first seawater greenhouse was built in 1992 on the Canary Islands, just off the northwestern coast of Africa.

A seawater greenhouse

? When was the first seawater greenhouse built? ________

# Save Water, Save Energy

**Water and energy are equally vital for human survival. Hydroelectricity, the most common form of electricity today, relies heavily on water. It consumes more water than any other energy source. Therefore, to ensure a sustainable future, it's crucial to use water wisely, recognising its central role in energy production.**

### More Demands on Water

Enhanced oil recovery and natural gas extraction methods, including hydraulic fracturing, are water-intensive processes. Water is crucial not only for extraction but also for processing and transportation. This highlights the significant demand for water resources in the energy sector.

### Energy Efficient Equipment

Water and energy can be conserved at home by using high-efficiency washing (HEW) machines, which consume 40% less water and 55% less energy than standard washers. Additionally, running full loads in the dishwasher saves about 37% more water compared to hand washing dishes.

**FUN FACT**

A tap left running for five minutes uses as much energy as a 60-watt bulb consumes in 14 hours.

### Water for Energy

Freshwater is essential for energy production. It's used in hydroelectricity generation and to cool power plants. Approximately 37 to 54 gallons of fresh water are required to generate one kilowatt of energy, depending on the type of plant. The volume of water used to cool power plants globally is comparable to the total water withdrawn for crop irrigation.

? Saving water saves energy. (True/False)

# Saving Water at Home

**It may not be possible to avoid using fresh water for domestic purposes altogether. However, unchecked use of fresh water for certain household activities leads to significant wastage. By fixing leaky taps, toilets, and pipes, one can easily save up to 300 gallons of water a day.**

## Domestic Sector

About 8% of the global fresh water is used for household and drinking purposes. In an urban household, about 90 gallons of fresh water are used daily for various activities like drinking, cooking, dishwashing, laundry, sanitation, and bathing. Another 5 to 10 gallons are used for gardening. To reduce domestic water wastage, people are encouraged to recycle water for sanitation and watering lawns.

## Faucets and Showers

About 15% of household water usage is from faucets. Using faucet aerators can prevent water wastage while washing hands by spreading water into tiny droplets. Replace standard showerheads, which use 2.5 gallons of water per minute (gpm), with water-efficient ones that use about 2 gpm. Consider using buckets for bathing to further minimise water wastage.

**FUN FACT**

A dual-flush toilet can save up to 67% of water in a household.

## Kitchen and Laundry

The tap should not be left running while washing vegetables or dishes by hand. Automatic dishwashers and washing machines should only be used with a full load. If running partial loads, adjust the water level accordingly instead of using the regular wash cycle that consumes the same amount of water as a full load.

? Which type of toilet has two separate tanks for flushing? ______________

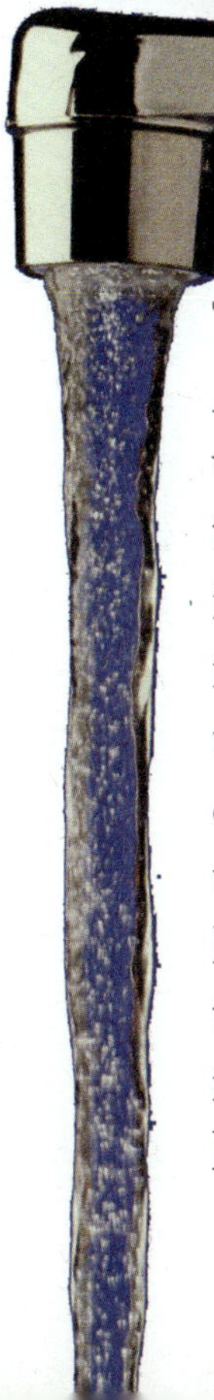

## Toilets

About 30% of household water is used for flushing toilets. To save water, consider installing low-flush or dual-flush toilets. Low-flush toilets use 1.6 gallons per flush compared to the 3.5 gallons used by conventional toilets. Dual-flush toilets feature two tanks—one with more water for solids and the other with less water for liquids.

# Saving Water in Schools

**Water is utilised for various purposes in schools, including drinking and cleaning floors. Given its numerous uses, adopting water-efficient practices is imperative to conserve this vital resource. It's essential to educate young children on water-saving techniques to prevent wastage.**

## Saving Water Outdoors

Schools can save significant amounts of water outdoors by:

- Planting drought-resistant plants and trees.
- Applying a layer of mulch around plants to retain soil moisture and reduce evaporation.
- Using a broom instead of a hose to clean school driveways, paths, and paved areas.
- Installing a rainwater tank and utilizing collected water for cleaning purposes.

**FUN FACT**

A dripping tap wastes approximately 1 drop per second, equivalent to wasting 7,000 litres of water per year.

## Saving Water Indoors

Schools can save significant amounts of water indoors by implementing the following measures:

- Replacing standard taps with automatic shut-off taps.
- Upgrading to dual-flush toilets that use less water per flush.
- Promptly repairing leaks.
- Installing aerators on taps to reduce water flow.
- Opting for mops rather than hoses to clean toilet blocks.
- Conducting quarterly inspections of all taps for leaks.

? Single-flush toilets should be replaced with double-flush toilets. (True/False)

# Waterless Technologies

**With increased awareness about the growing stress on freshwater resources and the need for water conservation, various waterless technologies have been developed to use water more economically. These technologies are particularly popular in arid regions and areas where water is scarce.**

### Waterless Urinals

Public waterless urinals eliminate the need for water flushing. They feature a hydrophobic chemical coating on their surface, enabling urine to slide into the sewer instantly. This coating also prevents bacterial growth and stains. Additionally, a non-returning valve in the drain prevents urine vapours from emitting foul odours.

### Waterless Washing Machines

Washing machines contribute to approximately 13% of a household's daily water usage. Waterless washing machines, however, operate without water. Instead, they utilise reusable nylon polymer beads resembling plastic beads to remove stains from clothing. These beads possess greater stain-absorbing capabilities than water. Following the wash cycle, the machine separates the beads into a drum, leaving behind clean and dry clothes.

### Waterless Car Washes

A traditional car wash consumes approximately 14 gallons of water, whereas waterless car wash technology cleans vehicles without water. It utilises a range of chemical products for cleaning. A unique wax is applied to the car's body, then wiped off with a microfiber towel, effectively removing tough stains from any surface.

**FUN FACT**

Waterless washing machines consume just one-tenth of the water and approximately 2% of the power used by conventional machines.

? What do waterless washing machines use to clean clothes? ____________

# Easy Ways to Save Water

**Tick the steps you take at home to save water:**

- Avoid letting faucets run unnecessarily while washing or shaving. ☐
- Ensure faucets are tightly closed when not in use. ☐
- Use water only when needed. ☐
- Minimise unnecessary flushing of toilets. ☐
- Take shorter showers to conserve water. ☐
- Use a sink or bowl to wash vegetables instead of running water. ☐
- Thaw frozen foods in advance or use the microwave instead of running water. ☐
- Choose water-efficient washing machines. ☐
- Sweep driveways and sidewalks instead of using a hose. ☐
- Avoid installing fountains unless water is recycled. ☐
- Water lawns during cooler times of the day to minimize evaporation. ☐
- Regularly maintain sprinkler systems for optimal operation. ☐
- Avoid over-fertilising lawns to conserve water. ☐
- Harvest rainwater for various uses. ☐
- Group plants with similar water needs together to avoid over-watering. ☐
- Use mulch to retain soil moisture. ☐
- Select drought-tolerant plants for landscaping. ☐
- Wash cars with collected water in a bucket instead of using a hose. ☐
- Use drinking fountains responsibly, releasing the button when not drinking. ☐
- Hand water small patches of grass; use sprinklers for larger areas. ☐
- Install rainwater harvesting systems. ☐
- Promote water conservation among peers and neighbours. ☐
- Bathe pets outdoors in areas needing watering. ☐
- Carry water bottles to minimise fountain use. ☐
- Raise awareness about water conservation. ☐
- Limit use of garbage disposals; compost food waste. ☐
- Plant in fall when rainfall is abundant. ☐

# Glossary

**Aerator:** a device for adding air to a liquid

**Aesthetic:** relating to beauty or art

**Alarming:** causing fear or distress

**Aquaculture:** the cultivation of aquatic organisms

**Arid:** dry, lacking rainfall

**Chlorine:** a chemical element used for disinfection

**Curb:** to restrain or control

**Debris:** scattered fragments, wreckage

**Distilled:** purified or concentrated through distillation

**Dripper:** a device that releases water slowly

**Efficient:** achieving maximum productivity with minimum wasted effort or expense

**Exquisite:** extremely beautiful or delicate

**Faucet:** a device controlling the flow of liquid

**Gravel:** small stones

**Honeycomb:** a structure of hexagonal cells made by bees

**Hydrophobic:** repelling water

**Impending:** about to happen, imminent

**Incorporating:** including as part of a whole

**Intrude:** to enter without permission

**Migration:** movement from one place to another

**Native:** originating from a particular place

**Percolate:** to filter gradually through a porous surface or substance

**Porous:** having small holes allowing liquid or air to pass through

**Recreational:** relating to leisure activities

**Relatively:** in comparison to something else

**Replenished:** refilled or restored

**Seepage:** the slow escape of liquid or gas through small holes or pores

**Semipermeable:** allowing certain substances to pass through

**Sensibly:** in a practical, reasonable manner

**Sensor:** a device that detects or measures a physical property

**Sieve:** a device for separating wanted elements from unwanted material

**Soaring:** rising very quickly to a high level

**Sole:** the underside of the foot

**Solvent:** a liquid substance capable of dissolving other substances

**Surcharge:** an additional charge or fee

**Thermoelectric:** relating to the direct conversion of heat into electricity

**Urbanisation:** the process of making an area more urban

**Valve:** a device for controlling the flow of a fluid

**Vicious circle:** a sequence of events in which each problem leads to another that makes the original problem worse

**Wetland:** a land area that is saturated with water, either permanently or seasonally, such as marshes or swamps

## Answers

Page 29 - Water crisis
Page 30 - About 97%
Page 31 - True
Page 32 - True
Page 33 - About 80%
Page 34 - Industrial
Page 35 - Drip Irrigation
Page 36 - In-ground sprinkler
Page 37 - True
Page 38 - Recycled Water
Page 39 - False
Page 40 - Distillation and reverse osmosis
Page 41 - Charlie Paton
Page 42 - True
Page 43 - Dual-flush toilet
Page 44 - True
Page 45 - Nylon polymer beads

# ORGANIC WAY

# Introduction

The rise in chemical pesticide, fertiliser, and herbicide usage has adverse effects on public health. This led to the emergence of the 'Going Organic' trend, gaining popularity in the 1970s. This approach advocates for a natural lifestyle, prioritizing the use of organic products whenever possible. It offers environmental benefits, notably reducing greenhouse gas emissions like carbon dioxide.

Organic farming consumes less energy compared to conventional methods, preventing soil organic matter depletion. It enhances nutrient cycling, curbs water runoff and soil erosion, and decreases pollutants. Thus, transitioning to organic products is a viable strategy to combat global warming.

# Organic Way of Life

**Embracing an organic lifestyle is an initial stride towards purifying the Earth from chemical exposure. It aids in eliminating toxic elements from the human body, promoting good health. Moreover, it can significantly contribute to addressing climate change and global warming.**

### Advantages

Organic practices minimise the reliance on chemicals in our everyday routines. Methods for producing food and other items organically exclude the use of pesticides, complex chemical compounds, or hormones. These resources are naturally sourced and are readily reusable and recyclable.

**FUN FACT**

Recycling batteries can reduce 165,000 tonnes of solid waste generated in landfills annually.

### Be Conscious

Educate yourself about the labels and certifications of organic products. This knowledge is crucial for distinguishing between organic and conventional produce. Enhanced awareness of organic production methods will inspire more individuals to embrace an organic lifestyle.

### Organic Expenses

Organic products are typically more expensive due to their unique, pollution-free production process. From cultivation to packaging, an organic approach is followed at every step, contributing to the higher cost.

? Organic products reduce the use of ______ in our daily lives.

# Organic Labels

**Organic labels and certification are rules created to determine if a product is genuinely organic. These regulations are overseen by various organisations in different countries, such as the United States Department of Agriculture (USDA) and the National Organic Program (NOP) in the US, and Bio Suisse in Switzerland.**

## Organic Certification

The process categorises products based on their organic content. Higher organic content means a more eco-friendly product. Those involved in producing or distributing organic goods must obtain certification.

## USDA

The USDA enforces standards from the Organic Food Production Act, 1990, resulting in four categories:

- 100% organic (carrying the USDA Seal)
- Organic (at least 95% organic components)
- Made with organic ingredients (minimum 70% organic)
- Natural (may or may not be organic)

## Other Labels and Certifications

Each country has its own method for certifying organic products. In France, ECOCERT provides certifications, labelling organic food as 'AB' and organic skincare as 'Cosmebio'. Germany uses Bio-Siegel labels, while Japan employs the JAS (Japanese Agricultural Standard) for organic products.

**FUN FACT**

Salt and water are not included in organic labelling.

? What does the USDA stand for? ____________________

# Organic Products

Chemical products harm human health and the environment. Organic products, produced eco-friendly and free from toxic substances, are a natural choice for many, prioritising health and the environment.

### Impact on Environment

Organic products, produced without chemicals, reduce pollution and greenhouse gas emissions. Their production involves less non-renewable energy, aiding in energy conservation.

### Impact on Biodiversity

A recent study acknowledges that organic farming fosters greater biodiversity compared to conventional methods. Harmful insecticides such as DDT adversely impact biodiversity by affecting the central nervous system of insects and other animals. Organic products aid in pollution control.

### Toxicity and Pollution Reduction

Only 1% of pesticides and fertilisers used for pest control benefit the plant, while the remaining 99% pollute the environment. Organic products avoid this issue by being chemical-free.

**FUN FACT**

Organic food remains fresh for longer periods without refrigeration.

*Pesticide being sprayed on an agricultural field*

? Which pesticide is harmful to the central nervous system of animals? ________

# Farming

**Organic farming aims for ecological balance through eco-friendly practices, avoiding chemicals, pesticides, fertilisers, and herbicides. It helps retain soil moisture, preserves fertility, and controls pollution, benefiting the environment.**

## Organic Farming Methods

Crop rotation, mulching, natural farming, and biodynamic farming are methods used in organic farming. Crop rotation alternates crops, while mulching retains moisture and adds nutrients. Natural, or do-nothing farming, pioneered by Masanobu Fukuoka, minimises tillage and irrigation. Biodynamic farming uses manures and composts as fertilizers, avoiding artificial chemicals throughout crop production.

## Maintaining Organic Farms

Organic agriculture encounters several challenges, with soil management being the foremost. Maintaining soil fertility is crucial, achieved through the addition of animal manure, compost, crop waste, and mulch to enhance organic matter content. Leguminous plants are grown to supply nutrients like nitrogen and potassium to the soil. Soil testing is advised to monitor fertility levels, allowing adjustments such as adding more raw or composted manure based on results.

*An organic farm*

**FUN FACT**

Sir Albert Howard developed the concepts of organic agriculture in the early 1900s, advocating for the use of animal manures, cover crops, crop rotation, and biologically based pest controls for a better farming system.

**?** Who introduced do-nothing farming?

______________________________

# Composting

**Composting is the recycling of organic matter, like animal manure and grass clippings, to create fertilisers. The resulting product, compost, is nutrient-rich and enhances soil moisture retention. It's a natural method of waste degradation.**

### The Composting Process

Composting is carried out by microorganisms, which break down long-chain compounds in organic matter and release nutrients. This process occurs either aerobically, in the presence of oxygen, or anaerobically, in its absence.

*Organic waste collected for composting*

### Vermicomposting

Vermicomposting utilises various worms to degrade waste. Red wrigglers, white worms, and other earthworm species are commonly employed for this purpose. These worms digest the waste and produce nutrient-rich worm castings, which are valuable fertilisers. Commonly used worm species for vermicomposting include red worms and white worms.

**Waste**

***Compostable items include:***

- Used egg shells
- Garden and pond plants
- Fruit and vegetable scraps
- Leaves and grass clippings
- Animal hair
- Shredded paper
- Soft cardboard

***Non-compostable items are:***

- Dairy products
- Meat
- Fish
- Dog excrement
- Diseased plants

*Vermicomposting*

**FUN FACT**

Earthworms can consume organic matter equivalent to their body weight.

? Animal hair is compostable. (True/False)

# Organic Horticulture

**Organic horticulture is the science of growing fruits, flowers, vegetables, and ornamental plants using organic methods. It relies on simple hand tools, avoiding chemicals and fertilisers. Plant growth is influenced by soil type, temperature, and rainfall.**

*Organic pomology*

## Types

Organic horticulture is divided into various categories:

- Organic floriculture: involves growing annual or perennial herbaceous floral plants.
- Organic landscape horticulture: focuses on cultivating floral species to enhance the beauty of an area.
- Organic olericulture: entails the cultivation of vegetables.
- Organic pomology: includes the cultivation, production, and storage of fruits.

## Useful Species

The choice of species relies on factors like soil condition and climate. Common organically grown vegetables and fruits include apple, melon, carrot, citrus, olives, grapes, cabbage, and cauliflower.

## Horticultural Rotation

Every organic method of crop production requires a balanced rotation. In an optimal horticultural rotation, deep-rooted crops should follow shallow-rooting crops, nitrogen-demanding crops should follow nitrogen-fixing crops, and so on.

*Organic vegetables*

**FUN FACT**

Horticultural rotation helps to control the spread of diseases and weeds in plants.

**?** The flower farming of annual or perennial plant species is called ________________.

# Organic Gardening

An organic garden comprises organically grown herbs, shrubs, flowering plants, and ornamentals. Essential practices include soil pH testing, adding compost and organic fertilisers, and controlling pests and weeds to ensure proper plant growth.

## Advantages

An organic garden offers an affordable, easy-to-manage, and readily available source of fruits and vegetables. It can be created to fit available space. Some vegetables, like carrots, are best grown organically as they absorb fewer pesticides compared to conventional methods.

*An organic garden with flowering and ornamental plants*

## Aims

The goal of organic gardening is to maintain the natural balance of the ecosystem. It emphasises minimal tillage to avoid environmental harm. Organic gardeners utilise organic fertilizers to nourish soil and plants, resulting in nutritious and safe produce.

*An organic nursery*

## Hydroponic Gardening

Organic hydroponic gardening is a cutting-edge method where plants grow in water instead of soil. They're nurtured in a plastic container filled with water and essential nutrients (N, P, O2, K, Ca, Mg) to aid nutrient absorption.

**FUN FACT**

Organic garden products contain 50% more nutrients than conventional farm products.

**?** In the hydroponic technique, ________ is used in place of soil to provide essential nutrients to the plants.

# Organic Food

**Organic foods are abundant in vitamins and minerals while containing low chemical concentrations. Consumption reduces the risk of various diseases. All organic food growers and manufacturers must adhere to government and international organic association standards.**

*Organic spices*

### Types

Organic foods are classified into several categories, including:

- Organic spices (cumin and garlic)
- Organic herbs (basil and neem seeds)
- Organic pulses and cereals (rice and bajra)
- Organic oil seeds (peanuts, yellow and black mustard)
- Organic/herbal tea (green tea)
- Organic dairy products (milk and cheese)
- Organic vegetables and fruits (cabbage and apples)
- Organic meat

### Cost

Organic foods are devoid of chemicals and typically cultivated in smaller quantities, leading to higher prices. While production costs may not be significantly higher, post-production expenses rise due to chemical-free treatment during harvesting, processing, and transportation.

**FUN FACT**

Conventional farming uses over 400 pesticides to combat various weeds, pests, fungi, and herbicides.

### Organic vs Non-Organic food

Regularly consuming organic food may help prevent cancer and heart disease due to their richness in phenolic compounds, antioxidants, and minerals. Additionally, they are fresher and often tastier than non-organic alternatives.

*Organic black mustard*

? Organic food is rich in nutrients and is good for health. (True or False)

# Animal Products

To obtain organic meat and fish, animals are raised without exposure to chemicals, pesticides, or growth hormones. They are housed in clean environments, with limited grazing space, and receive regular vaccinations. Organic meat is abundant in Vitamin E and essential fatty acids vital for the body.

Organic eggs

## Organic Dairy products

Organic dairy products, obtained from animals fed organic feed, include milk, cream, cheese, powdered milk, and organic ice cream. Organic milk is rich in Omega-3 fatty acids and Vitamin E. Organic cheese offers a blend of Omega-3, Omega-6, vitamins A, D, E, and beta-carotene. Organic lemon verbena and lavender ice cream are made with organic sugar, lavender, lemon verbena leaves, and cream.

## Organic Eggs

Organically reared hens, fed certified organic seeds, produce organic eggs. However, hens confined to "free-range" spaces may also produce organic eggs, but not consistently. Organic eggs are abundant in vitamins A, D, B9, B12, and B2. They also contain a high content of choline, essential for normal cell and nerve functioning.

**FUN FACT**

Organic meat tastes better than conventional meat.

An organic cattle farm

? Which fatty acid is found in higher quantities in organic milk? ____________________

# GE Food

**GE (genetically engineered) food is created by altering the genetic composition of plants, typically done in a laboratory to achieve desired qualities. Common modifications include resistance to pests and diseases, enhancement of nutritional values, and increased tolerance to cold temperatures.**

## Effects on Health

While most GE foods are considered safe, doctors and scientists worldwide remain uncertain about their long-term safety. In some cases, reports suggest that individuals have developed allergies after consuming certain GE foods.

**FUN FACT**

Organic farms maintain soil mineral levels over the years without leaching.

## GE or Organic Farming?

GE and organic farming offer contrasting approaches for the future. While organic farming aims for ecological balance and biodiversity, GE focuses on single issues, seeking technical solutions. For example, Bt maize targets maize pests like stemborers but may harm beneficial insects. Organic farming prohibits genetic modifications due to concerns about long-term impacts on consumers, soil, and the environment.

*Genetically engineered food*

*GE food has been reported to be allergic in some cases*

**?** Which is more nutritious and helps prevent diseases: GE or organic food?

# Health Benefits

**Consuming organic products is one of the easiest ways to achieve good health. Organic fruits, vegetables, and pulses are rich in essential nutrients like iron, phosphorus, Vitamin A, Vitamin C, and micronutrients. Organic meat is considered the healthiest form of meat.**

*Organic diet*

## Nutrition Level

Research indicates that organic fruits and vegetables contain 27% more vitamin content. Organic milk is a rich source of antioxidants. Food items such as organic carrot and coriander soup have higher levels of salicylic acid, which reduces swelling and may help prevent cancer.

## A Healthy Choice

Children, with their delicate tissues, are more vulnerable to toxins. Therefore, it's highly recommended to use organic food for them. Those who consume organic foods from an early age have lower chances of developing cancer, neurological disorders, and heart diseases.

## Is it Really Healthy?

While the environmental advantages of organic food are clear, its health benefits remain a subject of debate among scientists. Recent reports in newspapers suggest that organic foods are only partially free of chemicals, yet some research indicates they contain higher quantities of important nutrients.

**FUN FACT**

According to the EPA, nearly 60% of all herbicides, 90% of fungicides, and 30% of insecticides can cause cancer.

? To avoid accumulation of toxins, organic food is the best option for __________.

*Consuming organic fruit since an early age can fight off cancer and neurological disorders*

# Pesticides and Fertilizers

**Organic food is pesticide and fertiliser-free. In organic farming, pest, weed, and microorganism control methods must be organic. Homemade remedies like salt spray, garlic spray, flour, and buttermilk spray manage pests, while organic manure enriches the soil.**

## Organic Fertilisers

Organic fertilisers like manure, seaweed, peat, and worm castings provide essential nutrients to soils and plants. They reduce the risk of over-fertilisation, enhance soil nutrient storage, and improve soil structure while reducing erosion.

## Organic Pesticides

Organic pesticides are conventional compounds that control pests by disrupting their normal functioning. For instance, tobacco and nicotine spray can eliminate bugs, while plants like dandelion, Canada thistle, and plantain are used for weed control. However, some organic pesticides remain controversial, such as rotenone, copper, nicotine sulphate, and pyrethrums.

*Compost is used as organic fertiliser*

*Neem leaves are often use as pesticides in organic farming*

**FUN FACT**

The prolonged use of chemical pesticides damages the top soil.

**?** Name any two organic fertilisers.
1__________ 2 __________

# Clothing

Organic clothing uses materials from organic plants and animals, dyed with natural, chemical-free colours. These garments are eco-friendly, easily recyclable, and made from organic fibres like wool, cotton, and silk, available worldwide.

**Organic Wool**

Organic wool comes from livestock raised organically, fed organic food and fodder. Navajo-Churro sheep, a rare breed, are often used for organic wool production. Products made from this wool include baby clothes, blankets, and coats. Additionally, organic wool is naturally fire-resistant.

**Organic Bamboo**

Bamboo fibre is extracted through mechanical separation or heating processes. It is soft and highly moisture-absorbent, often used to make linen fabrics. Organic bamboo fabric clothes are versatile, suitable for both summer and winter wear.

*Linen fabric made of organic bamboo fibre*

**Organic Cotton**

Organic cotton is the most commonly used organic fibre, sourced from organically grown cotton plants. It is extensively utilised in personal care products, baby items, towels, bed sheets, and blankets.

**FUN FACT**

Every year, 20,000 deaths in developing countries are attributed to pesticide use in cotton farming.

? Which is the most commonly used organic fibre? __________________

# Furnishing

**Organic furniture is eco-friendly, crafted from non-toxic, renewable materials. Unlike conventional options, which may contain harmful chemicals, organic furniture is made from earth-friendly materials like reclaimed wood, recycled rubber, and recyclable plastic.**

Organic furniture

## Other Furnishing Items

Harmful chemicals found in mattresses and carpets, such as polyurethane foam and boric acid, can accumulate in the human body and act as desiccants. Therefore, it's recommended to use natural organic products like natural wool and natural latex instead.

## Environmental Impact

Organic furniture positively impacts the environment by using locally grown hardwoods, reducing imports and transportation emissions. Crafted from recyclable materials, it minimises waste generation and promotes resource efficiency. Moreover, incorporating recycled items in its production helps curb deforestation.

? ____________ is caused by volatile organic compounds.

## Toxins and Pollutants

Indoor air pollution stems from synthetic materials used in furniture, paints, and furniture polishes. Over time, these items release chemicals like radon, formaldehyde, and volatile organic compounds, which can harm the nervous system, especially in children.

**FUN FACT**

Between 1980 and 1995, deforestation affected nearly 2 million square kilometres of forest area.

# Cosmetics

**Beauty products are highly sought after as organic options. Developed from natural minerals and organic plant extracts, they avoid synthetic colouring or chemical compounds, making them beneficial for the skin. A wide variety of organic cosmetics are available today.**

*Cosmetics derived from organically grown rose*

## Advantages

Research suggests over 61% of popular lipstick brands contain lead, which is harmful to the skin. Organic cosmetics offer less exposure to toxic chemicals, devoid of artificial colours and other harmful substances. They are thick, concentrated, causing fewer skin irritations.

## Natural Cosmetics are Not Organic

'Natural' cosmetics, derived from plants, contain over 70% natural ingredients but may include synthetics. In contrast, 'organic' cosmetics are made solely from organically grown herbs, with at least 95% organic ingredients.

*Natural cosmetics obtained from plant products*

**FUN FACT**

One-third of all skincare products contain one or more potential carcinogens.

? Natural cosmetics are strictly organic in nature. (True/False)

# Organic Movement

**The organic movement aims to raise global awareness about organic farming methods and their adoption. Since the first half of the twentieth century, numerous organisations and individuals have been involved in promoting organic farming practices, driven by the belief in their sustainability.**

*Rachel Carson*

## History

Many individuals have played key roles in promoting organic farming. The term 'organic farming' was coined by Lord Northbourne in his book "Look to the Land" (1940). Sir Albert Howard, a British botanist, supported organic farming. Lady Evelyn Barbara conducted a pioneering experiment comparing organic and conventional farming, with results favoring organic methods. Rachel Louise Carson's book "Silent Spring" (1962) detailed pesticide effects, leading to DDT's US ban.

## Criticism

Critics argue that organic products are expensive and less accessible, while some claim organic farming prioritises freshness over taste. Nevertheless, supporters of organic products prioritise their health benefits over any drawbacks.

**FUN FACT**

**Americans are the largest per capita consumers of organic products.**

? Who is the author of the book *Silent Spring*?

____________________________________

*Field cultivated in organic manner*

# Projects

**Several countries have initiated organic projects to study organically produced products. Researchers involved in these projects study the growth conditions and nutrient requirements of various crops, as well as observe their impact on the environment.**

## Fiji Organic Project

The Fiji Organic Project aims to promote organic sugar, benefiting both the environment and the economy. As the island's economy relies heavily on sugar exports, the project aims to help Fijian sugarcane farmers transition to organic production methods, enabling them to tap into the growing organic market.

## Organic Farming in India

The Indian government has initiated a project to promote organic farming practices and reduce reliance on chemical fertilisers. This project involves providing financial and technical support for setting up units to recycle organic waste and developing markets for organic products. Additionally, it aims to raise awareness about organically produced products.

## Fallen Fruit Project

The Fallen Fruit project in Los Angeles promotes the sharing of fruits grown in public places, which are cultivated organically to benefit the environment and serve as ornamental plants. The naturally fallen fruits from the trees are collected at night.

**FUN FACT**

Consuming organic milk lowers the risk of Type 2 diabetes.

Organically grown fruits

? For which commodity was the Fiji organic project taken up? ____________________

# Baby Products

**Due to their delicate organ systems and increased susceptibility to chemical absorption, young babies are more prone to diseases. Hence, a variety of organic baby products—such as soaps, shampoos, food, lotions, mattresses, blankets, and toys—are increasingly used to reduce their exposure to harmful chemicals.**

### Baby Clothing and Bedding

Organic cotton or woolen clothes are recommended for newborn babies as they are soft and less likely to cause skin allergies. Similarly, using bed sheets and mattresses made from organic materials is advised as they are soft and do not release toxins into the air.

*Baby clothes made of organic wool*

### Baby Furniture

Organic furniture and accessories for babies are increasingly popular among supporters of the organic movement. They prioritise toxin-free environments for infants, opting for seats, cribs, and other products made from organic materials. Some stores even offer organic hammocks and beds.

### Baby Food

Organic baby foods, devoid of chemicals, minimise a baby's exposure to toxins, crucial for preventing any adverse effects on their mental and physical growth and development.

**FUN FACT**

Organic diapers made from natural materials are now readily available.

**?** Which common problem among babies can be avoided by using organic clothes and bedding?

# Glossary

**Aerobic decomposition:** breakdown with oxygen

**Antioxidant:** prevents degradation

**Bioaccumulation:** buildup of toxins in body

**Biodegradable:** easily broken down by microorganisms

**Biodiversity:** variety of organisms on Earth

**Cancer:** uncontrolled cell growth

**Compost:** fertile organic matter

**Conventional:** traditional method

**Chromatogram:** separation record

**Decompose/degrade:** break down

**Desiccant:** absorbs water

**Disinfectant:** kills microorganisms

**Environmental indicators:** show environment quality

**Fertilizer:** promotes plant growth

**Fibre:** thin cloth thread

**Flammable:** easily catches fire

**Filter paper:** filters impurities

**Fodder:** animal food

**Gene:** hereditary unit

**Groundwater:** water underground

**Herbicide:** kills weeds

**Hormone:** regulates growth

**Irrigation:** provides water to fields

**Leguminous plant:** adds nitrogen to soil

**Livestock:** domestic animals

**Mechanical separation:** separation by hand/tools

**Micronutrients:** required in small amounts

**Mulch:** topsoil cover

**Nutrient:** essential chemical

**Nutrient cycling:** movement through food chain

**Pesticide:** kills plant pests

**Pollutants:** harmful substances

**Reclaimed wood:** from used wood

**Recycling:** reusing products

**Resistant:** offers resistance

**Runoff:** water draining from land surfaces

**Sustainable development:** resource use to protect for future generations

**Tillage:** land preparation for crop cultivation

**Topsoil:** uppermost soil layer

**Weed:** unwanted plant competing for nutrients

**Worm casting:** nutrient-rich earthworm feces

## Answers

Page 51 - Chemicals

Page 52 - United States Department of Agriculture

Page 53 - DDT

Page 54 - Masanobu Fukuoka

Page 55 - True

Page 56 - Floriculture

Page 57 - Water

Page 58 - True

Page 59 - Omega-3

Page 60 - Organic food

Page 61 - Children

Page 62 - Manure and seaweed

Page 63 - Organic cotton

Page 64 - Indoor air pollution

Page 65 - False

Page 66 - Rachel Louise Carson

Page 67 - Organic sugar

Page 68 - Skin allergies

# Notes

# Notes